5 Secrets to Nail that Job!

N. HEMINGWAY

NIKE H SPEAKS LLC PUBLISHING

NIKE H SPEAKS LLC PUBLISHING

USA

ISBN 978-1-7377287-0-2

N. HEMINGWAY

This book is dedicated to my husband Bobby, my daughter Allisha, and my grandson Michael.

Thank you for all the hours you spent with me over the years, getting me ready for interviews.

I love you and appreciate you all!

N. HEMINGWAY

Contents

PREFACE 8

SECRET #1- LOOK THE PART 10

SECRET #2- TALK THE PART 12

SECRET #3- MIND YOUR MANNERS 16

SECRET #4- MINDSET 18

SECRET #5- SHOW YOUR BEST SELF 20

BONUS SECRET- 3 TYPES OF INTERVIEWS 22

CONCLUSION 26

APPENDIX 28

    LIST OF COMMON INTERVIEW QUESTIONS...................................28
    SAMPLE 'THANK YOU' EMAIL..30

Preface

In today's changing world regarding employment, landing your dream job (or any job for that matter) is becoming harder and harder. Some of us have to compete with a younger workforce, rapidly changing technology, advanced degrees, and companies that are downsizing just to name a few. While finding employment can be challenging, several tools can position you to rise above the other job candidates. One of those tools is mastering the interview process. This book will tell you about 5 secrets to nail that job!

N. Hemingway

August 1, 2021

Secret #1- Look the Part

We all know that looking professional is critical for interviewing. You want to make sure your interview suit is clean, pressed, and stain-free. Make sure that your shoes do not have any scuff marks, holes, or tattered shoelaces. Do ensure that your accessories (socks, shirt/blouse, pantyhose, tie, etc.) are well kept. Maintain your grooming, which includes hair nicely styled, beards and mustaches are neatly trimmed, and fingernails are clean and evenly filed. Ladies must wear neutral-colored nail polish, with nails not overly long. As far as make-up, ladies should strive for a natural look. Avoid bold or glittery make-up because that will be a distraction to the interviewers. You want their focus to be on you, your skills, and your experience- not on your appearance. You need to present a polished and professional appearance at a moment's notice, so it is good to designate 1 suit exclusively for interviews. You can change up the shirt/blouse or tie, so you want to keep this interview uniform as I call it, prepared at all times in case you get a call today for an interview tomorrow. When you look good, you come across more confident because you feel good.

Do not wear dangling or sparkling earrings. Gentlemen- please take yours out. Keep your jewelry to a minimum. Allow 1 ring per hand, and if the ring is flashy (i.e., bling), do not wear it. There have been several times where I have worn an older wedding ring because my current one is noticeable. Avoid wearing sparkly bracelets and necklaces as well. Pearls are always in style- they give you an elegant and classy look. You *can* wear that power suit that makes a statement, but you do not want to wear anything that detracts from your skills, talents, and abilities.

I was living in Phoenix, AZ at one time, and had an interview with a health care organization. I was dressed in a nice and expensive suit, while the interviewer was dressed in leggings, an oversized t-shirt, and thong sandals. The interviewer remarked on how nice I looked and stated that I should be doing her job. Needless to say, I did not get the job, but I looked the part. My husband works in the highway construction industry, and the typical work uniform consists of jeans, work boots, and a t-shirt. He had an interview several years ago in Washington, DC where he wore a button-down shirt with a tie, slacks, and dress shoes. The owner of the company was so impressed with his appearance, that he offered my husband a job on the spot! So no matter if you work in an industry that is dirty or requires physical labor, you can still present a polished and well-groomed professional at your interview.

Secret #2- Talk the Part

You want to be prepared for your interview so that you come across as competent and capable of doing the job. Part of this preparation is researching the organization and the job duties. You want to know the mission and vision of the organization, along with the desired skillsets the company is looking for in the candidate. Know the duties of the job that you currently have, so that you will be able to describe concisely what you do. Make sure you know your skills such as computer software, foreign languages, and communication (verbal and written). For example, you can say that you know Microsoft Word at an advanced level, Microsoft Excel at an intermediate level, and Microsoft PowerPoint at a beginner level. Make sure you are honest in evaluating your skills because you do not want to get in a position that requires advanced knowledge, and you only have beginner knowledge. You will be found out!

Knowing responses to common interview questions is very important. If an interviewer asks you, "Why should I hire you?" and your answer is, "Because I think I can do the job," then you have just blown that interview. Potential employers want to know what skills and experiences you are bringing to their organization. You should answer this question by briefly highlighting your background in the industry, your experience, and your interest in the position. Another common interview question is, "Tell me about yourself?" This is not where you tell the interviewers that you have 3 kids, 2 dogs, and you live in your momma's basement. The interviewers do not want to know your personal business. This is where you highlight your skills such as detail-oriented, flexible, team player, and organized to suggest a few. You can list 5-7 skills on this question. When answering interview questions, be brief and make sure your answers line up with the questions asked.

I was a senior in college, and being in your last year of college, you are cocky and think you know everything. Well, I interviewed with a local bank for an open position. The interviewer called me a few days later to inform me that I did not get the job. She also told me that I was dressed appropriately, but struggled to answer some of the interview questions. I made it a point to go to the library and start researching information about interview techniques. No, the world wide web (www) was not around when I was in college. I looked at books on interviewing tips and resume writing, which has helped me over the years to stand out from the crowd.

To make sure you are confident in answering questions during the interview, practice your responses. You can do this by having a friend or family member ask you questions, or by practicing your responses in front of a mirror. I cannot tell you how many times I stood in front of a mirror practicing my answers. By practicing in front of a mirror, I could see my facial expressions, hear my tone, and check out my posture and body language. You definitely want to make sure you have the right expression on your face. You can practice your smile and make sure you maintain eye contact while looking in the mirror. I tell my friends that they can wake me up from a deep sleep, ask me a common interview question, and I can rattle the answer off as if I was wide awake. This is where you need to be no matter what industry, you should have prepared answers to common interview questions that do not really vary.

You *ALWAYS* want to ask at least 2 questions during the interview. Asking questions shows the interviewers that you are interested in the organization and the position. One question you ask could be, "What skills did you value in the person that previously held this position?" This way, you can find out what skillsets the interviewers are looking for, and highlight these in your 'thank you' note or email. Another question you could ask is, "What is your leadership style?" This will give you an idea of whether that person is a micromanager (authoritative), a coach (motivational), or a hands-off person (delegates to others) just to name a few leadership styles. From these 2 questions, you can get a good idea if this company is a good fit for your personality and skills.

I took a position within the federal government where everyone was so nice and polite during the interview. But on my first day of work, my colleagues were telling me that they were not going to help me, train me, or give me data. My colleagues were in a power struggle with the supervisor, and I was a casualty of their conflict. Even though I asked all the right questions during the interview, I ended up in a position that did not fit my personality. It took me a year to transfer to another office. So asking questions during the interview is very important. Not only do you want to be a good fit for the organization, but you want to make sure the organization is a good fit for you.

Secret #3- Mind Your Manners

Interviewing etiquette is key. This includes smiling, saying 'thank you,' shaking hands with a firm grip, thanking the secretary/receptionist that checked you in, and sending a 'thank you' email or note after the interview. You need to send your 'thank you' note or email within 24 hours of your interview. It is best if you send the 'thank you' email or note on the same day of your interview. This will keep your name at the forefront of the interviewers' minds.

There are sitting protocols for an interview. After you shake hands with the interviewers, make sure you are invited to have a seat. I was on an interview panel at one time where the candidate just sat down after he shook our hands. This is a no-no. You are a guest, so let your host invite you to a seat before you sit down. Once you sit down, make sure you have good posture. Place your bottom to the back of the chair. This will cause you to sit straight up. Do not sit at the edge of the chair. This can cause you to lean forward or become off-balanced. Your feet should be flat on the floor. Ladies- you can cross your legs at the ankle.

Gentlemen- you can sit with your legs slightly apart. Do not cross your legs at the knee- this is not appropriate sitting for an interview. How you sit during the interview is part of your manners, so make sure you mind them well because a polite interviewee is a productive employee.

Secret #4- Mindset

Your mindset has to be one showing confidence in your abilities, skills, and talents. Showing a winning and positive attitude is part of your mindset. You have to pump yourself up by thinking you are the perfect candidate for the position, your skills and experience are exactly what the organization is looking for, and you will be an asset to the team and company. If you are sitting in the interview with your arms folded, hunched over, and giving lackluster answers, then your mind is not in the game of winning and landing the job.

My team and I were interviewing an applicant a few years ago who had a negative mindset. The person was slouched in the chair and gave half-hearted answers to the questions. Needless to say, she did not get the job. We found out later that the candidate did not want to work in our industry, but her father was able to secure an interview for her. She was not displaying a winning mindset, and it showed throughout her interview. Showing a positive mindset lets the interviewers know that you will embrace changes, value the mission and vision of the organization, and will follow company rules and policies. You want to project competence and confidence, and this starts with a mindset of positivity.

Secret #5- Show Your Best Self

This is the part of the interview where you show the interviewers you are a team player, you are flexible, you are dependable, and that you have leadership qualities to name a few. You are displaying all of your positive characteristics, along with outlining your skills and abilities to your potential employer. When I interview with a company, I make sure that I highlight my skills and experience when I answer some of the common interview questions. I also restate my reasons for being the best candidate in my 'thank you' email or note.

Showing your best self during the interview also involves good manners. I have a friend who is the secretary in her office and acts as the gatekeeper during the interview process. She would place different kinds of emojis on the applicants' resumes, such as a smiley face, sad face, or mean face to name a few. Once the candidate was done with the interview, the director would come out and discuss with her the emoji on the resume. If a candidate were rude to my friend, the director would not have that person back for a second interview. So it is important to be polite to everyone you come into contact with because you do not know if their input is used in the hiring process.

Your dress is part of showing your best self. You do not get a second chance at making a first impression. If you are dressed in a suit that is clean and well kept, then you will have that extra boost of confidence walking into that interview. Your outer appearance indeed affects your inner appearance or mindset. Your mindset has to be confident and upbeat so that you display your best self to others. You always want to show your best self during and after the interview.

Bonus Secret- *3* Types of Interviews

Now that you know the 5 Secrets to Nail that Job, I want you to be prepared for different types of interview settings. Some interview environments you may encounter are in-person, telephone, and virtual/online. I will briefly discuss each and how you can successfully navigate each one.

The **in-person interview** is where you see the interviewers face-to-face. Do not be surprised if you are interviewed by 2 or more people. Panel interviews are common these days because teams will block off the whole day to just interview applicants. I have personally been interviewed by a panel consisting of 6, and have been on a panel composed of 10 interviewers. If you go in expecting a panel interview, do not be put off if you are interviewing with only 1 person.

Make sure you are dressed professionally for your in-person interview. Since you are having direct contact with the interviewers, it is important that you present a polished and well-groomed appearance. You can wear that power suit that makes a statement, but wear a standard color such as black, navy, or brown.

Your appearance as a well-dressed professional will help set the tone in your interview.

You will prepare for the in-person interview just like any other. You will do your research on the organization and the job applied for. Make sure you know the answers to common interview questions. Make sure your answers reflect your experience and the skills required for the job. Arrive at least 15 minutes before your scheduled interview time. This will give you a chance to settle in, go over the job description, and get your mindset right. Arriving early will also benefit you if the interviewers finish with the applicant ahead of you, and decide to call you in before your scheduled time. The in-person interview allows you and the interviewers a chance to gauge each other's personalities and if you are a good fit for the organization.

The **telephone interview** is another setting you may encounter in your job search. This type of interview is conducted over the phone. You will not be able to see the interviewers, nor they you in this type of environment. So do not worry about being dressed professionally. You still want to prepare for this type of interview just like you did for the in-person. Make sure you are prepared by doing your research beforehand on the company and position. You want to make sure your tone during the interview is positive and upbeat since the interviewers will not be able to see your facial expressions or body language. This is why a winning mindset is so important.

For the telephone interview, your environment is key to making a good impression. Get in a quiet space, where there are no loud noises or talking. You do not want to be distracted during this time. Have your hands free- put the call on speaker. You want to be able to take notes, especially the responses you get regarding the questions that you ask. For this type of interview, you can have your answers to common interview questions in front of you. Make sure you do not rustle pages where the interviewers know you are looking at responses. Do not depend on your paper to answer these questions- always be prepared!

As with the in-person interview, the telephone interview can consist of a panel of 2 or more interviewers. Each person on the panel normally introduces themselves, and the role they have with the organization. It is ok to write down their names; do not be overly concerned about getting their titles. Expect each person on the telephone interview panel to ask you questions about the position, your skills, etc. Ensure that you are available 15 minutes before your scheduled interview time. After you get on the call, please put your phone on silent so that you will not be interrupted by incoming calls. Remember that the telephone interview is sometimes used as a screening tool for companies. If you dazzle the interviewers on the phone, this typically leads to an in-person or another telephone interview.

The **virtual or online interview** is the last interview type I will discuss. This type of interview involves you being on the computer, tablet, or cell phone. The interview can be conducted via Google Meet, Microsoft Teams, Skype, or Zoom to name a few of the popular video conferencing platforms available. Once you get the meeting invite and accept it, you want to make sure you download the appropriate meeting application.

Just like the in-person interview, you still need to dress professionally (at least from the waist up). Make sure your grooming is well done, along with wearing neutral make-up and nail polish for the ladies, and trimmed beards, mustaches, and fingernails for the gentlemen. Your appearance for the virtual/online interview is just as important as if you were there in person. A well-dressed candidate makes a good first impression during an interview.

The virtual/online interview can consist of a panel of 2 or more interviewers. Again, people's time is valuable, so a team will typically interview job applicants as a group. With the different meeting stages being used, do not be surprised if team members pop in and out of your interview as their schedules permit. Remember- keep your poise, confidence, winning mindset, and manners intact. I have been on interview panels where the director or company owner has popped in during the interviews to ask candidates a few questions. If you are prepared for your interview, then unexpected "surprises" will not rattle you.

Conclusion

Let us take a look at what you need in order to nail that job:

1. <u>Look the Part-</u> You want to look professional by being well-groomed from head to toe. If you are not happy with your appearance, it will show in how you conduct yourself during the interview.

2. <u>Talk the Part-</u> You want to be competent in how you answer the interview questions, as well as asking questions about the company and the position you are interviewing for. If you are not confident in your answers, you will find yourself stumbling in your responses, and this is not good.

3. <u>Mind Your Manners-</u> Being polite is important. I am from the South, and we like to say, "Good manners will take you a long way." This is so true. Smiling and eye contact are part of interviewing etiquette. You want to show that you are approachable, friendly, and paying attention to what is being said during the interview. I cannot stress enough that a polite interviewee is a productive employee.

4. Mindset- Having a positive attitude and showing confidence, will let the interviewers know you are confident in your skills and abilities and will value the organization's mission and vision. If you do not show a confident attitude, then how will the interviewers be confident that you can do the job? Mindset matters!

5. Show Your Best Self- This is your time to shine! You want to let the interviewers know your strengths, your skills, your manners, and how you will be an asset to the organization. Showing your best self will put you at the top of the list of candidates, if not landing the job.

Whether you are just starting your career, a seasoned career veteran, or in a career transition, interviewing well is a must. Interviewing is a skill that you can master over time. It took me several years to become proficient in interviewing, so I know it can be done successfully. It takes practice and dedication to become a competent and confident interviewer. You have to look the part, talk the part, mind your manners, have a positive mindset, and show your best self in order to nail that job! Your resume gets you in the door, but your interviewing skills will keep you in the room. The 5 secrets that I shared with you, along with the bonus secret of the 3 interview types, will give you the edge you need to be successful in nailing your first job or your dream job.

Appendix

List of Common Interview Questions

Write these questions down on a separate sheet of paper, and write down your responses underneath each question. Then practice your answers.

1. Why should I hire you?

2. Tell me about yourself?

3. What are your strengths and weaknesses?

4. Where do you see yourself in 5 years?

5. What would your supervisor say about you?

6. Tell about a situation where you assisted a co-worker. What was the situation? What was your involvement and what was the outcome?

7. Describe a major change you have made in the past two years. How did you accomplish the change? What difficulties did you encounter and how did you work through the difficulties? What personal factors assisted you in making the change? Would you do anything differently if you had to do it again?

8. Describe a time where you were able to effectively communicate a difficult or unpleasant idea to a superior. What made your communication work?

9. Give two examples of things you have done in previous jobs that demonstrate your willingness to work hard?

10. Give an example where you used good judgment and decision-making in solving a problem?

Sample 'thank you' email

Make sure you highlight your skills and experience and how you will be an asset to the organization. This is where you show your best self!

July 12, 2021

RE: Public Health Analyst Position

Dear John:

I would like to thank you and the others on the interview panel for taking the time today to interview me regarding the Public Health Analyst position. My background in public health, my experience managing multiple public health programs for underserved populations, and my interest in the Public Health Analyst position will equip me to handle the work. I have an excellent track record of establishing and maintaining effective working relationships with diverse groups, along with my excellent verbal and written communication skills where I write reports and represent upper management at meetings as needed. I will be an asset to XYZ organization because I bring my organizational skills, interpersonal skills, and leadership skills.

Thank you for your consideration of my credentials, and I look forward to hearing from you soon.

Best regards,

Jane Smith

Made in the USA
Columbia, SC
10 February 2023

12140723R00017